Gaucholand Boy

Gaucholand Boy

The Frank Westphals in South America

by Barbara Westphal

Pacific Press Publishing Association
Mountain View, California
Oshawa, Ontario

Cover art and inside illustrations by James Converse

Library of Congress Cataloging in Publication Data
Westphal, Barbara Osborne.
  Gaucholand boy.

  (Trailblazer)
  Summary: Memoirs of the family of the first Adventist minister to
South America, before the turn of the century.
  1. Missions—South America—Juvenile literature. 2. Seventh-day
Adventists—Missions—South America—Juvenile literature. 3. West-
phal family—Juvenile, literature. [1. Westphal family. 2. Missionar-
ies. 3. Seventh-day Adventists—Missions—South America] I. Title.
BV2851.W47   266'.673 [B]   81-14079

ISBN 0-8163-0454-8   AACR2

Dedicated to
the great-grandchildren of
Frank H. Westphal
Carl's grandchildren—Gabriela, Patricio, Diego,
and Marie
Grace's grandchildren—Kent, Tiffany, Heidi,
and Brent

Preface

This book is another in the series of books for the young child, to acquaint him or her with some of the men and women who were trailblazers for Christ in Seventh-day Adventist history. Ellen G. White says that we have nothing to fear for the future except as we forget how God has led us in the past. The purpose of these books is to acquaint our boys and girls with the men and women who have followed Jesus and pioneered the way in God's work, both here in our country and across the sea, and to show the boys and girls of today how God has led in the past.

This series is the result of the desires expressed by many church-school teachers for extracurricular reading and enrichment in their church-school programs.

It is the hope and prayer of the publishers that these books in the Trailblazer series will assist the children in becoming acquainted with God's leaders and His work, enriching not only the young child's knowledge, but his reading and comprehension skills as well.

The Publishers

Acknowledgment:

For these stories I am indebted to
F. H. Westphal's book *Pioneering in the
Neglected Continent* (Nashville, Tenn: Southern
Publishing Association, 1927), as well as to
anecdotes remembered by members
of the family.

Chapter 1

Carl pushed the oatmeal around in his bowl with his spoon as he sat at the breakfast table. He just didn't feel like eating. He wished Father were at home. Suddenly he pushed his bowl away and frowned. "Mother," he asked, "isn't Father ever coming home?"

Mother Westphal stopped eating. She smiled as she pushed Carl's bowl back in front of him. "In another week he'll be home," she said. "I know it seems like a long time since we've seen him."

Carl's frown deepened. "I miss him. Why does he have to be away so much and for so long at a time?"

Mother reached over and touched Carl's arm. "I miss him too," she said. "But you know, Son, he has a very important work to do here in South America. He is the first and only Seventh-day Adventist minister in all of the country. Only one Elder Westphal for a whole continent!"

Carl sat up straight. The frown left his face, and he smiled. "I hadn't thought of that." He picked up his spoon and began to eat his oatmeal.

"I don't suppose you remember," Mother said, "how lost we felt when we first came to the city of Buenos Aires four years ago."

11

"Not really. I was only four years old," Carl answered.

Mother went on as if she hadn't even expected Carl to answer. "We couldn't speak Spanish. We didn't know where to buy bread and milk, or how to go to town. We had only been here one week when Father had to go off to Entre Ríos [En-trā Rē-ōs]."

"I remember I used to cry when Father went away," Carl said. "I felt afraid without him around." He paused and then added sadly, "We had baby Helen with us then, remember?" He looked over at Mother and saw her wipe tears from her eyes. Then he saw her try to smile. "Mother is sure brave," he thought.

"Our friend the book salesman helped us learn where things were," Mother said softly. "Now you and I know pretty well how to get along even though Father isn't with us, don't we?"

"We have to help him with Spanish words." Carl laughed. "He is always preaching in German, so he doesn't learn Spanish as quickly as we do."

Mother began to stack the dishes. "You are certainly a big help," she said. "Children always learn a language so much faster than grown-ups."

"Spanish is easy," Carl boasted.

Mother laughed and ruffled Carl's hair. "But English is not, and we want our son to read it and write it well. We'll get right at our lessons before I have to get at the office work."

Carl sat at the table with his chin cupped in his hands. He sat there for some time while Mother rinsed the dishes. Suddenly he asked, "Mom, why did Father have to go away so soon after we got here? Why couldn't he have stayed with us and helped us get settled? It doesn't really seem fair."

"Son," Mother spoke up quickly, "you know why your father was sent here to South America. There was no Seventh-day Adventist minister in the country; and a certain German-speaking family, who had become Adventists in the United States where they first lived after leaving Europe, came to Argentina. They were the only Adventists in this area."

"You mean the Riffels?" Carl asked.

"Yes, the Riffel family. When they left the States and came to Argentina, they began to tell their friends about the seventh-day Sabbath and about the second coming of Jesus. They talked a lot about Bible teachings, and their friends wanted to know more. So the Riffels wrote to the General Conference and asked for a minister."

"Who could speak German," Carl interrupted.

"That's right." Mother Westphal nodded. "And the General Conference sent your father. And of course, that meant we came too. When we arrived, the Riffels asked Father to come to Entre Ríos right away. Your father answered that call."

Carl began to laugh.

"What's so funny?" Mother asked.

"I was remembering the story Father told about his first night. He had taken a ship up the Paraná [Pa-ra-ná] River to find the German settlement where the Riffels lived. Remember?"

"Yes," Mother nodded. "That first night he slept on the ship, but on the second night the ship docked near a small town. No one had come to meet him, but he spied a big hay wagon and decided to climb into the wagon and ask the driver to take him to a hotel. So he got off the ship and got into the hay wagon. The driver of the wagon must have been very surprised. Your father asked him to drive to the hotel, but the man couldn't understand English. When Father spoke in German, the man couldn't understand that either. But at last he realized that your father wanted to go to a hotel. He slapped the horses on the back with the reins and drove up the steep hill to the hotel." Mother Westphal paused and smiled at Carl.

"And the next morning," Carl began, "Father found a man who spoke German and asked him if there were any Adventists around."

"Imagine how surprised your father must have been when the man told him there were lots of them," Mother said.

"Oh, but the next part of the story is really funny." Carl laughed. Father stayed at the house of a German farmer the next night. The farmer gave him a big sheepskin coat to use as a blanket. He wrapped himself in the coat and lay down on the floor in the kitchen to sleep. He said the wool felt good around his neck at first. But it must have seemed strange to have the ducks and geese and chickens all sleeping in the same room with him." Carl stopped talking and giggled. Then he said, "Can't you just imagine Father beginning to scratch as he lay there all wrapped up in that big sheepskin coat?"

"I guess it really wasn't funny at the time," Mother Westphal said. "But, yes, I can imagine father lying there itching and scratching. That coat was full of fleas!"

"I know! I know!" Carl went on. "He finally threw

the coat off and got up and went outside. But it was so cold he had to walk fast trying to keep warm. His own clothes were now full of fleas too. So he kept on scratching."

"Poor father," Mother said. "He didn't get any more sleep that night. He had to go inside because the dog started to bark, and he didn't want to wake up the farmer and his family."

"Well, that trip was a success," Mother went on, "because as soon as word got around to the farmers in that area, they all came to hear Father preach the next night. And he preached half the night. The people were so interested they didn't want to go home. He preached three sermons that night. It was one o'clock in the morning before the people went home."

Father had stayed for several days, Carl remembered. "He baptized thirty-six people before he came home from that first trip."

Mother nodded. "That's right," she said. "That was the beginning of the Crespo [Krés-po] Church, the first Seventh-day Adventist church in all of South America. That church grew rapidly. Now there are 200 members."

Carl was thoughtful for a while. Then he said, "Mother, I'm glad we came to South America as missionaries. We are doing what Jesus wants us to do—telling others about him."

Chapter 2

Mother stood by the little kerosene stove boiling the milk for the day, when Carl asked, "Mother, how much money does Father make?"

"What a question! That's not something that a child needs to know." Mother kept stirring the milk. "We have enough to live on. No money for any extras. But at least it comes every month now."

"Didn't it always come every month?" Carl asked with surprise.

"No, Carl, I remember when we left New York four years ago, Elder Olsen handed us our tickets and $170. It was all the General Conference could spare at the time. We didn't know when they would send more. You see, Father was the very first minister sent to South America. They didn't have very good plans then for taking care of missionaries."

The milk began to boil, and Mrs. Westphal took it off the stove just before it spilled over the edge.

"Remember when we didn't have enough money for the milkman when Helen was a baby?" Carl asked.

"Do you still remember that? You were only five years old!" Mother looked at her son standing beside her.

"Sure, I remember because it has always been my job to wait for the milkman every morning," Carl said. "I always sit on the doorstep holding an empty pan. I listen for the cowbell. Soon the milkman walks around the corner leading his cow right down the street. When he comes to our house, I jump up with the pan, give him the coins for the milk, and wait while the milkman milks the cow right there in the street. He makes two warm streams of milk take turns splashing into a big pan. Then he measures the milk and pours it into our pan." Carl paused. "I remember the day when there were no coins for the milkman. Baby Helen was sick. We had prayed that we could get milk. You said there was a ship coming in that day. Maybe it would bring money from the General Conference."

Mother smiled and hugged Carl. "Yes. Father told us to stay at the house and pray while he went to get the mail. How we prayed that day." Mother went on. "Poor baby Helen cried and cried. I'm sure Father must have been praying too as he went to the post office."

Mother and Carl were quiet for a few minutes. Then Mother said, "How sad Father must have felt when the postman told him there was no mail."

"Father told me he prayed again," Carl said. "After that prayer, a man in a blue serge suit stepped up to him and asked if he was a missionary. Father nodded Yes, and then the man said, 'Good. I would like to invest some money. I want to invest in a missionary.' "

Mother now went on with the story. "Yes," she said, "but Father told him he couldn't make any

2-G.L.B.

money on him because he had none in the first place. But it was really strange what happened next. Because the man told Father he would let him know a year in advance when he wanted his money. Then he handed Father a thick envelope."

"Father said his hands trembled as he took it," Carl spoke up quickly, "and in the envelope was $150 in bills!"

Although Carl knew the story by heart, he asked, "And then?" He loved to hear this story over and over.

"Father shut his eyes to pray, and when he looked up to thank the man in the blue serge suit, he was gone," Mother answered. "And although he searched from house to house for the man, he never found him. And do you know, Father believes, and I believe too, that it was an angel who gave him that money."

Carl opened his dark eyes wide. "My father saw an angel!" he said softly.

Mother smiled at Carl. "Yes. It could very well have been an angel. We certainly believe it was."

Chapter 3

One day Carl, who had been studying in the room that he and Mother used as a classroom, slammed his book shut and frowned. "I don't like to be an only child. I don't like to go to school all alone at home. And I don't like to have my father always away!"

Mother Westphal, who had been sitting at a desk writing, looked up at Carl. She put down her pen and went over to her son. "But you should feel proud of your father. He is in charge of the East Coast Mission in South America," she said, placing her hand on his shoulder.

"What does that mean?"

"That means that he has half a continent to look after. The two big countries are Brazil and Argentina. Then there is little Uruguay between them, and Paraguay far up the river Paraná. He must visit them all."

Carl thought a minute then said, "Brazil is really big, isn't it?"

"Larger than the United States," Mother answered. "Carl, do you remember that Father was in Brazil when we lost Baby Helen?"

"Yes," the boy answered. "At least I remember he was away from home. That was the year after we came to South America and I was only five."

Mother Westphal sighed. "Baby Helen was only a year and a half when she got sick. She'd been sick for several weeks when Father had a call to go preach in Brazil."

Carl remembered very well now how sick Baby Helen had been. She had had the measles. Then both Baby Helen and Carl came down with scarlet fever.

"It must have been very hard for you to take care of both Baby Helen and me," Carl said. "I was very sick, I remember."

"Yes, Son, you had a high fever and didn't even know what was going on for several days. You just lay there in bed, tossing and turning. Then one day you opened your eyes and asked for a drink. I was so happy, but I couldn't help crying. I brought you a drink of fruit juice. And I thanked God for sparing your life." She gave Carl a squeeze.

"But little Helen—" Carl began and then paused.

"Little Helen had fallen asleep, never to waken till Jesus comes," Mother said, and wiped the tears from her eyes. Then she smiled. "Carl, do you remember asking then where your father was? You asked if he was also gone until Jesus would come. Father was away for five months that time."

"Why didn't you write to him and tell him we needed him?" Carl wanted to know.

"I did. Several times," Mother Westphal answered.

"When Father came home he saw how sad I looked. He saw your pale, thin face, Carl. He looked for the baby. She wasn't there. He guessed what had happened."

" 'Little Helen died two weeks ago,' I told him, beginning to cry. 'Oh, I've been so lonesome!'

"Father was surprised that I hadn't written.

"I told him I had written several times. He never got those letters. Together the three of us went to the cemetery. We took flowers to Helen's little grave. How glad we were, Carl, that God had spared your life. It will be a happy day when Jesus comes," Mother told Carl. "Helen will wake up. An angel will bring her to my arms. Then we will all go to heaven together."

Upon his father's return home after a long trip, Carl loved to listen to his stories of adventure. Father Westphal often had to travel by foot or by muleback. One time when he had to go by ship, he had no money for a first-class ticket, so he had to sleep in a bunk with no mattress or blanket.

Carl would settle himself comfortably in his father's lap while he listened to the stories about the trip. Mother would sit nearby with her sewing basket so she could mend Father's socks while she too listened.

There were a few Sabbath keepers near a small town in Brazil called Brusque [Brüs′kā] when Father first went there. No minister had ever been there to tell them about the Sabbath.

"How did they hear about the Sabbath?" Carl asked when Father began to tell about his trip to Brusque.

"They first heard about the Sabbath because someone sent papers in the mail. A sailor on a ship had said to a missionary that he wished someone would send a certain magazine to his stepfather.

21

The missionary got the stepfather's name and address and sent the magazine.

"The stepfather got ten copies of the magazine in the mail. Fortunately the magazine was in German. The magazines came each month. The stepfather gave the magazines to others to read. You see, there were many German-speaking people in Brazil.

"A certain man who wanted money to buy whiskey said he would sell Adventist papers. He took them from house to house among the German families. Sometimes he was very drunk! Once when a lady opened the door, he fell right into the house! But people read the papers. They studied the Bible. They began to keep the Sabbath.

"So I visited the little group near the town of Brusque. No one would rent me a house for the meetings, so we met by the river. There the people sat on logs. We had the Lord's Supper out of doors. For a table they used a flat log and laid the bread and the wine on it.

"I baptized eight people in the river one Thursday and fifteen more the next Sunday. That made the very first Seventh-day Adventist church formed in all of big Brazil.

"On the last night there was a man who asked me to go to his house for a meeting. He had invited his friends. It was a hot night. I stood with my back to an open window. As I preached, I begged the people to get ready for Jesus' coming.

"Suddenly there was a noise like the firing of a gun. The people caught their breath. Then they began to pick up stones from the floor. I turned around to see where the stones came from. A big stone was caught in the lace curtain at the window. It was right behind my head.

"The owner of the house fell on his knees.

" 'Pastor Westphal,' he said, 'God took care of you. I saw eight men outside that window. They all had stones in their hands. One of them counted to three. One, two, three. Then they all together threw the stones at your head. Only God could have saved you.'

"We all knelt down then to thank God for His protection," Father added.

One day Carl asked his father why he didn't learn to speak Spanish the way he and Mother did.

Father laughed. "Just as soon as I have time, Son. You see, I am always visiting German and Swiss people, and I preach to them in German. I haven't had a chance to pick up much Spanish. But I do get into a lot of trouble by not knowing the language better."

"Like the time the gauchos pulled the knife on you?" Carl asked.

"Gauchos! Oh, yes, that is the Spanish word for *cowboys*, isn't it?" Father asked and winked at Mother. "This is gaucholand, isn't it? At least Brazil has a lot of gauchos."

"Yes, both Brazil and Argentina and some other countries in South America have gauchos." Mother laughed. "I guess you are a gaucholand boy, Carl."

"You know," Father began, and Carl knew there was a story coming, "I remember the time I started for a little town called San Xavier [Sän Hä vyăr]. I didn't arrive until 11 o'clock at night, a very dark night. I had no idea where to find a hotel. But I began walking. I couldn't find a hotel anywhere. At last I got onto a country road. I saw a light flickering in the distance. Of course I headed for that light.

"I found two men crouched by a fire drinking a kind of tea that is called mate [mä tä].

"I asked the men, who were gauchos, where I could find a hotel. But they couldn't understand me. They said something in Spanish, and I couldn't understand them. So I just lay down near the fire, using my bag for a pillow.

"When I awoke, I found I was surrounded by gauchos and horses. The gauchos were wearing long loose pants gathered together at the bottom. Instead of belts they wear sashes, and always there is a big knife hidden in the sash.

"One of the gauchos pulled out his big knife and pointed it at me."

Carl's eyes were as wide as saucers. "Oh, Father, what happened then? Weren't you scared?"

"Well," Father answered, "I didn't feel very comfortable. I sent up a silent prayer asking God to protect me. And do you know, that gaucho must have realized I had no gun. He put his knife back in his sash.

"I tried to ask the men how to get to the home of the family I wanted to visit. At last they seemed to understand; at least they heard me mention the family's name several times, so I guess they understood. One of the men pointed in the direction I should take and talked very fast in Spanish.

"I finally found the family, and while I stayed at their home, I held meetings for all the German, Swiss, and English settlers in that town."

Chapter 4

Carl always hoped that some day he could go on a trip with his father. His father had promised that one day Carl could go with him.

"Father, when are you going to take me on a trip with you?" Carl asked when his father came home from one of his trips.

"I'd like to take you, Son." Father paused, then he added, "Sometime when I make a short trip perhaps. Or sometime when Mother can go along."

Mother must have heard Father Westphal, for she suddenly spoke up. "Frank, you know I can't get away. I have to be treasurer and Sabbath School secretary for this big mission. Every day I work in the office besides teaching Carl."

"Yes, Mary, that's true," Father answered. "I don't know what I would do without your help. If you didn't work, I would have to stay home myself." Then he turned to Carl. "There is one place where I'd especially like to take you, Carl."

"Where's that?" Carl asked.

"To the Chaco [Chä' kō], Son. That's gaucho country like our wild west in the United States. I'd like to take you to visit the Kalbermatter family. They live on a big ranch, and there were seven boys in the fam-

ily when I was there three years ago. There may be more now."

"Could I ride horseback with them?"

"You certainly could. Those boys ride all day over the pampas, that's what they call that area, it's grassland, a prairie. Don't you remember the story I told you about the baptism in the well?"

Carl laughed. "That was funny!"

"No," Father corrected him. "It was a very solemn meeting. Well, I'm glad we now have another minister in South America. Elder and Mrs. Town are coming over this evening. I'm going to tell them some of the experiences I've had in this country. By the way, Mary, with their help it may not be long until you can get away from the office. It's great to have another minister here now."

That evening when the Towns came to visit the Westphals, Carl could hardly sit still while he waited for his father to begin telling the experiences he had had in South America. Carl loved to listen to the wonderful stories of how God had protected his father and how the people accepted the story of Jesus.

At last Father Westphal began to tell things that had happened to him and to the people when he brought the story of Jesus to them.

"Mr. Kalbermatter," he began, "is a Swiss farmer with a big ranch. An Adventist book salesman gave him a book to read. After reading it, the rancher wrote and asked to have a minister visit him. He wanted to learn more about the Bible. That's why I went to visit the family.

"The first evening we settled down around the big

kitchen table to study the Bible together. Mr. Kalbermatter and his sons were all smoking pipes.

"Next morning when I studied with them again, I told them tobacco was bad for their health. I explained that God wanted them to keep their bodies pure and clean.

"Then I went outdoors to pray. I asked God not to let them be angry. I was afraid they would not stop smoking. I was afraid they wouldn't want to study the Bible anymore, but when I went back to the house, Mr. Kalbermatter met me with a smile and told me to look up at the rafters in the house.

"I looked up, and what do you suppose I saw? All the pipes hanging above me. They were tied in a bunch up there under the roof.

"Mr. Kalbermatter said that they couldn't reach the pipes and they would not smoke nor would they drink whiskey anymore. He also said he wanted me to baptize him and his sons.

"I knew they needed to study much more of the Bible first. So every day I taught them in the morning and in the evening. And every once in a while he would ask if they could be baptized now. And I'd always tell him they needed a few more Bible studies.

"They were happy until I studied about paying tithe. Mr. Kalbermatter didn't want to pay tithe. He got very angry and said I was only after their money. The next morning he said he would hitch up the wagon and take me to the station. I could leave right away.

"I said I wanted to say Good-bye to the boys who were out in the field.

"When I found them, I told them that their father

wanted me to leave at once.

"The boys didn't want me to go. They wanted to be baptized first.

"I went back to the ranch house and told Mr. Kalbermatter that I would find another place to stay. I told him his sons wanted to be baptized before I went away.

"He seemed very surprised that his sons wanted to be baptized. He didn't say anything for a moment. Then he spoke up saying that if his boys wanted to be baptized, he would be baptized too. He also said he would pay the Lord His tithe."

Father Westphal paused in his story. Then he smiled and went on. "I bowed my head and sent up a prayer of thankfulness," he said. "But how could I baptize this family? We Adventists baptize as Jesus' disciples did. We need lots of water. The water must be deep.

"When I told that to Mr. Kalbermatter, he said they had lots of water on the ranch.

"I had seen no lake or river. But Mr. Kalbermatter said he knew where there was plenty of water. And took me to the corral and showed me a well with a small opening. But below, the well spread out and filled a space like a room. The water was very deep.

"I told him that this water was *too* deep! I told him I was only five feet eight inches tall and he was shorter than I. The water would be over our heads. But Mr. Kalbermatter assured me he could fix that.

"On Sabbath we had a short meeting. We sang and prayed. Then Mr. Kalbermatter slung a rope over a pulley on a cross beam in the corral. He tied one end to a huge bucket like a tub. Then he had me stand in the bucket. As he and some of the others held the rope, they let it down, with me in it, into the well. A valve let water into the huge bucket. When the water came up to my waist, Mr. Kalbermatter fastened the rope above so the bucket would not go down deeper in the well.

"One of the boys was lowered by another rope. When the boy was beside me, I baptized him. His brothers pulled him up. That way the boys and their father were all baptized.

"They are a great family. I think the boys will be missionaries someday." Father Westphal ended the story.

"I certainly am anxious to visit that family," Elder Town said.

"Yes," Elder Westphal agreed. "I'm sure your duties will soon take you to the Chaco."

"And what about me?" Carl asked. He couldn't give up his dream of going out into the country with his father soon.

Chapter 5

One evening after putting Carl to bed, his parents talked quietly together. Mrs. Westphal said, "Frank, there's no money to pay the rent. And I don't have enough for food either. What shall we do?"

"Let's pray about it." That was always Elder Westphal's first thought.

Together they knelt down. Each one told the Lord they needed money.

"Dear God, we try hard to make the money last. We never waste a penny on things we don't need. But we do need to buy food and to pay our rent. Please send us help."

When they got up from praying, the Westphals went to bed.

The next morning when Mother Westphal opened the door, she saw a piece of paper stuck in a crack beside the door.

"It's a letter!" she said out loud.

Father and Carl hurried to look.

"That's a funny place for the mailman to leave a letter!" Elder Westphal said.

Mother opened the envelope up fast. Two bills fell out.

Carl picked them up. He looked at the numbers in

the corners. "One hundred pesos [pā sōs]!" he shouted. Then, "Another one hundred pesos!"

His mother turned the letter over to see from whom or where it had come. There was a signature. "Brother Kalbermatter."

Father said, "God certainly heard our prayers the night before."

"Did you pray for money last night, Father?" Carl asked.

"Yes, Son, while you were asleep."

Father Westphal said it was a miracle to find the bills inside the letter. "Bills mailed inside letters are always stolen," he explained.

"God took care of it for you," Carl said.

It wasn't the first time. Carl knew that the family had needed money since the time the man in the blue serge suit had helped them.

He remembered the time that Father had written to Elder O. A. Olsen, president of the General Conference at that time, and told him about their need. When a letter came back from Elder Olsen, Father had been very happy. But when he opened it, there was no check inside. Father had read the letter out loud. "We have no money to send you," it said. "You are just as near God in South America as we are here. Ask Him."

Once when Father had to make a trip to Uruguay across the river, he had been praying hard for money but hadn't said anything to anyone about it.

A friend by the name of Mr. Hugo, who had a cheese factory, asked Father right out if he needed money.

"Yes, we surely do," Father had answered.

33

Mr. Hugo pulled forty pesos out of his pocket. "Take this," he said, "and I'll give you forty more next time I see you."

Soon after that Carl heard his father tell his mother that Mr. Hugo had died. "Too bad he never paid tithe," Father said. "He always intended to, but he felt he didn't have enough money. He left a lot of debts. Now Mrs. Hugo has all those debts to pay. She has decided to pay tithe first." Father paused and Carl saw a happy smile come over his face. "I am sure God will bless her because she plans to give God a tithe of all she has," he added.

And God did.

Once, during a revolution in Uruguay, a band of robbers passed through the country stealing horses and cattle.

Mrs. Hugo had a beautiful horse worth a thousand dollars! She didn't want the bandits to find her fine horse. But where could she hide it? Of course, the thieves would go right to the barn. So she decided to hide the horse in the house! Her home had three rooms arranged in a row. Carefully she led her horse up onto the porch and then through the front door. She guided her horse into the end room. She saw that the curtains were well closed. Gently she patted the horse, telling him to be quiet. She left the horse there and went back into the middle room and pushed a heavy dresser against the door. How she prayed that her horse wouldn't make a sound! He mustn't stomp his feet. He mustn't whinny. The horse never made a sound.

The bandits searched through the barn and the cheese factory, and the house—all but the room that had the heavy dresser against the door, but they never found the horse.

Later she sold the horse and sent all the money to help in Adventist mission work.

"God saved the horse for me. God kept the horse quiet. Now the money is for Him and His work," Mrs. Hugo said.

Chapter 6

One day Father came into the room where Mother and Carl were busy with Carl's schoolwork.

"How would you both like to go with me to visit the German families in Entre Ríos?" he asked.

Carl slammed his book shut and jumped up from the chair. "At last! At last I'm going!"

"Oh, do you think it would be all right for me to leave the office work now?" Mother asked.

"Yes, of course. This time I'll take both of you with me." Father gave both Mother and Carl a hug.

"Father, I know that Entre Ríos means 'between rivers,'" Carl said, "but is it really like an island with rivers around it?" he asked.

"The rivers go almost all the way around the province," Father explained. "But it's such a big place you won't feel as if you were on an island."

They traveled on a riverboat up the Paraná River just as they knew Father had done for the first time four years before.

Carl spent hours on the deck looking over the rail. Their ship was a side-wheeler. The great wheels on the sides of the ship looked like waterwheels. The paddles went round and round, lifting and splashing the water.

"This is the kind of boats we have on the Mississippi River in the United States," Mother told him.

Before they reached the port, Mother said she would have to open their trunk to get out some more clothes that she had packed away.

Carl and his father went with mother to get the clothes from the trunk.

"Frank, the trunk is open! Mother exclaimed as she bent over to unlock it. "I'm sure we had it locked," she gasped.

She lifted the lid. "The clothes are gone. Stolen!" Then she added, "And we have so little money for buying more."

"Well," Father said, "we'll just have to rely on God who has promised to supply all our needs."

"And that's just like Father," Carl thought to himself.

When they arrived at the port, there were some of the new Adventists there to meet them. Carl remembered how his father had climbed into a hay wagon on his first visit and had tried to tell the driver where to take him. Now those who met them were their friends. It was easy to see these people loved father. They welcomed his family with love too.

These friends had brought several wagons to the port. Two strong horses pulled each wagon. Carl and Mother and Father rode in one of the wagons to the Riffel family's home. Instead of talking Spanish with the children, Carl began talking German. Instead of being called Carlos in Spanish, he was now Karl, spelled with a *K*.

One day Mother said to Carl and his father, "You know, there are children everywhere here, but there is no school. I'm going to start one right away."

But there were no books, no desks, no paper. One of the families who had an extra room let Mother have school in their home. The children had slates to write on. For books, they had the German Bible and hymnbook.

Carl begged to go to school too.

"Well, Carl. We'll forget the English lessons for a few weeks. You will learn to read and write German instead. Most of the children are older than you. I hope you can keep up with them."

Carl made himself as tall as possible. "I'm eight years old. Of course I can keep up," he said.

One day Carl came into the schoolroom where his mother was correcting papers. "My father isn't afraid of anything," he said.

"What do you mean?" Mother Westphal asked. "Did something happen at the meeting you were attending with your father?"

Carl took a deep breath. "Yes," he said. "Three bad men came into the meeting place. One had a revolver, one a long knife, and the other had an iron bar about four feet long." Carl stretched his arms out to show mother the length of the bar.

"They shouted for us to get out in ten minutes. They said they would be back to fight after the ten minutes.

"Father just kept right on preaching. The people kept right on listening, so I did too. Father didn't close the meeting until he had finished his sermon.

"The three bad men came in again. One carried his revolver, and the other carried the long knife. The third had that iron bar four feet long. We could tell they were angry. They shouted. Father just looked the three men in the eye. The three angry men began to tremble. Then they backed away and left."

"That sounds as if you were brave too, Carl," his mother said proudly.

"Father made us all feel brave," the boy explained.

"Father and God," his mother added.

A few weeks later Carl went to a baptism with his father. As they walked toward the river, a man came up to Elder Westphal and walked beside him. Carl knew it was one of those three bad men. He knew which one it was—the one who had carried the iron bar. He thought his father didn't remember the man. So he spoke to his father softly in English so the man couldn't understand.

"Father, be careful. This is one of those three bad men."

His father nodded to him. He knew who the man was.

After watching the baptism, the man said, "Pastor Westphal, I want to be baptized too. I'm not ready yet because I have been a very wicked man."

Carl wondered if such a wicked man could change and serve Jesus. But sure enough, at a later baptism the man was ready. Elder Westphal led him into the river. Raising his hands, he repeated the solemn words, "I now baptize you in the name of the Father, the Son, and the Holy Ghost."

Just then one of the man's old friends came up. He was the one who had scared the people with his revolver. Now he carried a bottle of whiskey. He came right to the water's edge. Tipping up the bottle, he took a big swallow of the whiskey.

"Good-bye, my friend," he shouted to the man just baptized. He meant they wouldn't have anymore drinking parties together.

"What a different path those two men have chosen!" Father said. "One will probably die a drunkard. The other will live a happy life of helpfulness to others."

Chapter 7

Carl looked out the window of the dried-mud house in Entre Ríos where he and his family were living. Locusts swarmed everywhere. On the road, on the grass, on the cornstalks. They swarmed around the house trying to get in through any of the cracks and crevices in the mud walls.

Carl turned from the window as he heard Mother call, "Here, Carl, take this broom and sweep out those locusts." She handed the broom to him.

"Ugh! They come in as fast as I can sweep them out. Mother, I *hate* them! They go crunch, crunch under my feet, and they smell horrible." Carl frowned, stepping on the ones that had slipped inside. "This is like the plagues of Egypt," he added.

"Yes," Mother agreed. "The first time your father saw a cloud of locusts, he thought he saw a rain cloud. He was in a wagon, and he told the driver to hurry. He wanted to get home before it rained. The driver told him that was not a rain cloud. It was a cloud of locusts."

"When will these things go away?" Carl wanted to know.

"They go away when they have eaten everything green. That won't take long. But before they fly away,

they lay their eggs in the ground."

"When do the eggs hatch?"

"The next season. The baby locusts are called hoppers. They can't fly, and they are almost white at first. The hoppers do as much damage as the adult locusts."

Mother Westphal looked out the window sadly. "Our friends will have no corn crop this year. We will have no apples or garden vegetables this year."

"And the little lettuce seeds you planted are just coming up," Carl remembered.

"Oh, they are gone already, Son."

"What'll we eat?" Carl asked, his voice a little shaky.

"Oh," Mother smiled, "Don't worry. We'll have beans and macaroni. God will supply our needs."

"And eggs," Carl added cheerfully.

"We won't enjoy eggs much for a while," Mother said, "The chickens eat the locusts. Then they lay eggs that have very red yolks that look bloody. But let's think of something more cheerful," Mother said, looking down the road. "I see Father coming. That must be Luis Ernst with him. Father doesn't know what to do with Luis."

Carl knew all about Luis and his problem. He remembered how Luis had first come to them. It was just after a series of meetings. Luis came with a bag in one hand and a book in the other.

Father Westphal exclaimed when he saw him, "It's Luis Ernst from Uruguay! I've met him before." Then he hurried to Luis. Carl heard Father say, "Luis! What brings you here?"

"I've come to go to school," the young man had

said. "I feel God has called me to be a minister. I want to study."

"But we have no school," Carl's father told him sadly.

"No school!"

Carl could feel how disappointed Luis was.

"I am sure God wants me to be a minister," he said slowly. "I sold my land and my cattle in Uruguay. My cheese factory I gave to my brother. But what can I do if there is no school?" Luis looked as if he were about to cry.

Luis said he had spent many days and nights praying. He had confessed all his sins. He had made things right with everyone. He had even remembered that as a small boy he had stolen five cents' worth of candy. He had gone to the storekeeper, paid for the candy, and had been forgiven. He now wanted to work for the Lord and he needed an education. What was he to do?

Carl wondered if he could be as honest as Luis, and if he could be that brave.

Now Father Westphal and Luis came into the house. Locusts came in too. Father picked up a broom and swept them away. Carl followed his father and Luis into the kitchen where Mother was.

"Mary," Father Westphal said to Mother, "I've decided what to do with Luis. I'll take him with me everywhere I go. I can teach him history, German grammar, and the Bible. He will give me Spanish lessons in return. Doesn't that sound like a good trade?"

And so after that Luis Ernst often stayed with the Westphals.

However, just now Carl had other things on his mind besides Luis Ernst. "Are we really going to eat macaroni and beans all year if we stay here?" he asked. "I think I'm ready to go back to the city—and get away from these horrid locusts."

Chapter 8

One day Carl came home soaking wet. He had been playing with neighbor children. Mother Westphal gasped as he came into the room dripping wet. "Carl, whatever happened?" she asked.

Carl looked down at the water dripping from his clothes and onto the floor. "I—I learned to swim," he said, hanging his head.

"With your clothes on?" Mother asked.

Carl shifted his weight from one foot to the other. "Well, I wasn't trying to learn to swim. A big boy pushed me in the creek."

"Carl, Carl, what were you doing to the big boy? Teasing him?"

"Well, maybe," he said looking down. Then he raised his head. "But it all turned out for the best, Mother. "I was so scared! And somehow I paddled to the bank. The big boy stood there laughing at me."

"Son, you could have drowned!" Mother said as she dried him with a towel and pulled off his soaked shirt.

"I think the boy would have pulled me out if I hadn't begun to swim," Carl said thoughtfully. "He's not a bad boy. I did tease him. But now I can swim! Now I will be a better missionary some day. Can I go again and practice some more?"

Mother laughed. "Well, yes, but not with your clothes on! And you'll have to have someone with you who knows how to swim well."

Carl also learned to ride horses bareback with the farm boys. He felt proud that he had learned so much in the country. At nine Carl was old enough to be helping his missionary father in many ways. One day as he stood by the door of a meeting place where he had been helping to arrange the benches, an officer with two soldiers came up to him and handed him a paper. "Give this to the preacher, my boy," the officer ordered.

Carl took the paper to his father. Elder Westphal read it and looked troubled.

"It is an order from the judge," he said sadly. "He says we can't have a meeting here."

When Elder Westphal told some of his friends, they said they would go and talk to the judge. They brought back the news that the judge had given permission to go ahead with the meetings, but they couldn't have a baptism.

Elder Westphal conducted the meetings every day. On the second Sabbath he announced that they would have a baptism that afternoon.

Somehow the officer must have heard about it, for he came with the soldiers again. He told the missionary, "If you have a baptism, I will take you to the judge as a prisoner."

"Then you might as well take me prisoner right now," Father answered. "No," the officer said, "I can't take you now because you haven't had the baptism yet."

Carl felt afraid that afternoon. Would his father be taken to prison?

Father did go ahead with the baptism. Seven people were baptized.

"I will go to the judge myself Monday morning," Elder Westphal told the officer.

"All right," the officer agreed, and went away with his two soldiers.

True to his word, Elder Westphal went to the judge Monday morning. When he returned home, he told Mother and Carl that the judge said his officer had told him that the baptism was a beautiful service. "He said the people that I baptized wore modest clothes."

"What did he expect?" Mother asked.

"He thought they would be naked."

Carl had to laugh at that, but Father was telling more. "The judge asked me if we believed in obeying the laws of the country. And of course I told him we did. I said that the Bible teaches us to obey the government. Only we must obey God first."

"What did he say to that?" Carl wanted to know.

"He said, 'Good! That's right.' "

"Did the judge really think the people you baptize don't wear any clothing?" Carl asked then.

Father nodded. "Someone must have told him that. People do get strange ideas sometimes." Father Westphal laughed.

Chapter 9

"Let's get at our English lessons," Mother Westphal said one morning after putting the last of the breakfast dishes on the shelf. They were living in the city once more. They had been away from Entre Ríos for several months.

"I don't feel like studying these days. I have so many headaches," Carl grumbled.

"I know, Son. And I don't feel like teaching you either. I guess we both ought to see a doctor. But let's not give up. You are doing well in Spanish and in German. We want you to keep up with English also."

"Well, I'll try, but I'm really tired of school. I wish we were in Entre Ríos again. I had a good time while I was there helping Father. I keep wondering how the school that you started is coming along."

Carl knew that since Luis Ernst had appeared, Father Westphal had been talking to everyone about starting another school. After nine months of talking, Elder Town, who worked in the office in the city of Buenos Aires decided to leave the office and begin a school in Las Tunas [Läs Tü' näs]. Of course Luis Ernst went right there to study. But the Adventists in Entre Ríos wanted the school to be there. They hoped they could buy land there. And at last a man gave them 40 acres of land, and other farmers promised money from selling part of their wheat crops.

The farmers hauled the bricks that had been bought to the place for the first building. But since all the money had been spent on bricks, there was no more for building. So Elder Town and Elder Westphal went to work themselves, and they took Carl and Mother along. Father Westphal carried the pails of lime to the men who were laying the bricks. Elder Town was the cook. Carl carried water and ran errands. Father told him he was most helpful.

Carl knew his father and Elder Town were most anxious to have a good well. They had hired a well digger. While he dug, the two ministers carried away the dirt. When the well was forty feet deep, the well digger stopped working.

"I won't go any farther down," he said. "I've struck soft dirt. It might cave in on me and bury me."

What would they do without a well digger?

Just then Luis Ernst came to visit. He asked how the work was going.

"We have a problem," the men told him. "Our well digger won't go down any farther. We need the well. Without water, we can't keep on building."

Luis Ernst walked away. He went to the other side of the pile of bricks. Carl heard his voice. The boy went closer to peek.

There was Luis kneeling on the ground. He was praying, "Dear Lord," he said, "You know You called me to be a minister. I have to go to school. They are building a school but they need water. There is no one to dig the well. If You will take care of me, I will go down into the well. I will dig it."

So Luis began to dig. Carl spent a lot of time standing at the top of the well watching him. Also he helped haul the dirt away.

They knew that soft dirt could slide down and bury Luis. Sometimes at night the soft dirt did slide down. Then Luis had to dig it out again the next morning. But God took care of Luis when he was in the well.

He dug down twenty-five feet farther.

"Water!" he finally called up.

The men all rushed to see. Luis dipped his hand down and tasted a few drops.

"Clear, good water!" he yelled up to them.

They lined the whole well with bricks. How happy they all were for that good water!

Carl and his mother had to leave Entre Ríos and go back to Buenos Aires. He kept thinking about the new school. Luis Ernst would be the first student. He was sure of that. He wondered if he, Carl Edgar Westphal, would someday be a student there also!

Chapter 10

Carl hadn't been fooling when he complained of headaches. He wasn't trying to get out of his home classes. As the days and weeks went by, both Carl and his mother felt worse.

Then one day his mother announced, "Carl, we are going home! Home to the United States!"

"Oh, I can't believe it. When do we leave?" he asked.

"In a few days. But it isn't all fun, Carl. Father isn't going with us. Just you and I are going. We need some medical care we can't get here."

"Oh." Carl's voice changed from glad to sad. "I'll be sorry to leave Father. I hope we can come back real soon." Carl paused a moment. Then he smiled and went on, "But there's one thing I can't wait to do. And that's to go to a real school with other boys and girls. I hope I'll be well enough to do that right away."

"I don't blame you, Carl," said Father, coming into the house as Carl was talking. "Missionary children make lots of sacrifices. But you've been so lucky to have an excellent teacher in your mother."

"His 'excellent teacher' hasn't felt like teaching for a long while." Mother smiled. "But I hope I'll be able to come back quickly to you, Frank."

Then turning back to Carl she said, "We'll see your grandparents on the farm and all the uncles and aunts and cousins."

"Mother, I thought we were never going to see them again. You told me we came to South America for the rest of our lives."

"Yes," she answered. "That's what we expected. And when we get well and come back, it may be for the rest of our lives—or until Jesus comes."

Father Westphal spoke up, "The six years we've been in South America have been good years. We've seen God's work grow and grow."

"You've worked in Brazil and in Uruguay and here in Argentina," Carl said. "Why haven't you ever gone to Paraguay? Isn't that part of your field?"

"Indeed it is, Son. I have wanted to go. Just haven't had the time."

Mother spoke up. "You haven't been feeling well either, Frank. Always with that red rash on your swollen face! You should be going home with us. Surely the doctors in the United States would find out what causes it."

"Oh, I can't get away from my work," Father said quickly. "But speaking of Paraguay, Carl, let me tell you something I just heard about how the bandits treated a missionary there."

"Oh, what did you hear? A bandit and a missionary?"

"A missionary family had been living in Paraguay for a time," Father began. "They had not been able to make any friends. There were many enemies who wanted to drive them away. A mob gathered around their house. They pounded on the door until they broke it down. But the missionaries ran out the back door and got away.

"The mob took everything the missionaries had. They divided it between themselves—the dishes, clothes, chairs, beds. There were many books too, but no one wanted them. Most of the mob couldn't read. Then one of them had a bright idea.

" 'Let's give these books to our leader's wife. She knows how to read, and she likes good books.'

"Even the bandits knew those books were good!" Carl laughed.

"So the wife of the bandit chief got the books," Father went on. "She began to read them. More and more she read. Soon she became a Christian—a Seventh-day Adventist Christian.

" 'These are good books!' she told her husband. He read them also."

Carl made a guess. "And he gave his heart to Jesus too!"

"Right," Father said.

Father turned to Mother. "Mary, when you get home, you tell our people that when we came to South America, there were no baptized members, and now there are more than a thousand, 250 of them in Argentina."

Carl felt very proud of his father. Of course he knew the book salesmen and the other ministers had done their part. But he knew his father had worked hard. He never seemed to meet anyone without beginning to talk about Jesus' return.

Carl was ten years old when he and his mother sailed back to the United States. The year was 1900.

Father Westphal didn't stay long in South America without the family. The very next year he was so ill that he too went back to the United States. The family lived in Nebraska at Union College where Elder Westphal taught German.

While they were in the United States, they visited many churches and camp meetings. Everyone wanted to know about their years in South America.

To Carl it seemed strange that so many people asked him about Indians.

"Mother, why do all the people ask me about the Indians in South America?" Carl asked one day. "When I tell them I never saw an Indian, they are so surprised."

"Well, Son, of course there are plenty of Indians in the highlands of Peru and Bolivia. Many people seem to think that the continent of South America is the same all over."

Carl said it was very strange that Americans didn't know more about the other America.

As his father told stories, other people decided they wanted to be missionaries in South America. One of these was Elder Westphal's younger brother, Elder J. W. Westphal. When Carl heard that Uncle Joe and Aunt Jennie were sailing to Argentina, he felt excited. Perhaps some day the two families could live near each other. Uncle Joe had a boy, Arthur, about Carl's age and a girl, Flora, a little older.

Nearly four years passed before Carl's family returned to South America. Carl's wish to be in a real school with other boys and girls had come true. He didn't think he would need special classes in English anymore.

Carl liked the way American children called their father "Daddy." It sounded close and loving to him.

"Father, couldn't I call you Daddy? So many children here in America call their fathers that."

"No, no, Son. That is something very new, and I don't think the best people say it. To me it doesn't sound respectful," Father Westphal said. "I like to be called Father."

That was that. Carl kept on saying "Father." After all, it too was a beautiful word.

Now Carl had a baby sister once more to make the trip back to South America with them. Ruth Evangeline was a sweet little blond almost a year old before they left the States. When they sailed back to South America, Uncle Joe met them at the port. Carl picked him out of the crowd at the dock immediately. He was taller than his father, and he had a long curly red beard.

"Where's my cousin Arthur?" Carl wanted to know at once.

"He and Flora are going to school at the academy in Entre Ríos," his uncle told him. "We live there, and you must come and visit us."

That was exactly what Carl wanted to do.

After a few days in the capital city of Buenos Aires the family took the riverboat up the Paraná River. What a welcome they received from their friends in Entre Ríos! Carl could see that his father had a very special place in their hearts since he had been the first one to give them the Bible truths. And what a fuss all the old friends made over the new baby!

Carl and Father and Mother felt very happy to see the training school doing so well.

"Come with me to school tomorrow," his cousin Arthur suggested.

"I'd like to go to school with you, not only tomorrow, but every day," Carl answered. "But I'll have to go and live wherever Father's work is going to be."

"I'm lucky to be able to live at the academy in the country," Arthur said. "But, my father's work isn't here. He is in charge of the South American Union Mission in Buenos Aires. That means that he travels most of the time. That's not so good. We hardly see him. He is away for many months at a time."

A missionary doctor had also joined the work in Entre Ríos—Dr. Robert Habenicht. Carl noticed how busy he was.

"Father, I've been thinking," he said thoughtfully. "I think I would like to be a doctor. What would you think of that?"

"Fine, Carl, fine. As long as you are helping others get ready for the coming of Jesus. I think being a doctor would be an excellent way to help the people.

Carl had forgotten many Spanish words during the years he had been away, but they came back to him rapidly. But where would the family live? This was his biggest problem.

Chapter 11

"Carl, your mother and I have decided—" Father paused.

Carl dropped the book he was reading and came to instant attention. What had they decided? Did they know now where they were going to live?

"Well," Father continued in his gentle way. "The committee has asked me to go to Chile."

The boy's heart sank. He knew Chile was a fine country, but he did wish he could stay at the academy and go to school with his cousin Arthur. Of course that was too much to expect. A missionary must go wherever he is sent.

"You see my face is already red and swollen as it used to be. Perhaps in Chile I shall be free of this problem."

"When do we go?" Carl asked slowly.

Mother spoke up. "Father is going by ship. He is taking the long way around. That way he can do missionary work along the way. The Falkland Islands will be his first stop."

"The Falkland Islands! That's where the whaling ships go. Those islands are out in the Atlantic Ocean! That isn't exactly on the way to Chile," Carl said.

"It's the route the ships take. And that way Father can leave Christian books there and talk to people. Then the ship goes through the Straits of Magellan and then—"

"The Straights of Magellan!" Carl exclaimed. "Where the terrible storms are?"

Father said the storms come as ships go around the island of Tierra del Fuego, around Cape Horn at the tip of South America. He said it shouldn't be especially rough through the Straits. That is a short-cut. Then the ships sail north along the Pacific Ocean up the coast of Chile. He would go to the port of Valparaiso [Väl pär ī' sō] in Chile.

Carl found his geography book while Father talked. Now he followed the route on the map. He was beginning to like the idea. "I'll really be seeing exciting places," he said.

"But we aren't going with him, Carl," Mother explained. "Not until he gets settled in Valparaiso or finds a place for us to live. In fact we have decided—"

There was that word again! What had they decided?

"—to stay here a few months so you can have a whole school year here at the academy," Mother finished the sentence.

Carl slammed his geography book shut. "Whoopee! "That's great! I'll study hard."

"Good, Son." Mother seemed pleased too. "Then you and I will cross the Andes Mountains with baby Ruth and join Father in Chile."

Carl couldn't have been more pleased.

That year Carl studied hard at the academy. It

seemed the year flew by, and soon he and Mother and baby Ruth Evangeline were on their way to Chile and Father.

Carl was anxious to hear about his father's long trip around the tip of South America.

"The journey through the Straits of Magellan was very interesting," Father said. "The pilot had to know the route well. There are many islands and many channels. He doesn't know which way to go except by a map. I often wondered how Magellan found his way through it."

Carl thought it must have been full of ice and snow and glaciers, but Father reminded him that it was springtime. You know the seasons are just the opposite here to what they are in the United States. Summertime there is wintertime here and so on."

"Punta Arenas [Pün tä Ă rē'nas], meaning Sandy Point, is the southern most large city in South America. There are thousands and thousands of sheep on those cold plains. I wanted very much to stay and hold meetings, but I had to travel on with the ship."

"I suppose you will be wanting to go back there to preach, won't you?" Carl asked.

"Yes, indeed, Carl. I hope I can go back there very soon."

When Elder Westphal first came to Valparaiso, he thought the people looked at him strangely. He said he didn't know whether it was because of his red face or his funny Spanish. The rash on his face cleared up after he left Argentina. And in Chile he found himself speaking more and more and better and better Spanish.

There was a little print shop in Valparaiso where

the Spanish *Signs of the Times* was printed. Carl and his mother went with Elder Westphal to visit the shop and meet the people who worked there.

When Mother Westphal saw the mission office and the printshop, she said, "This old place is a firetrap, Frank. Do you have it insured?"

He had to confess it was not insured.

"In case of fire, it would be hard for the workers to get out through these long dark hallways," Mother said. "And the street is too narrow for a fire wagon, I think."

The very next day Father said he would see about insurance on that old building in Williams Passage. "Come along, Son," he said to Carl.

Carl put on his good clothes and they started out. They went from one insurance office to another. Every time Father said the office was in Williams Passage, the insurance agent would throw up his hands and exclaim, "That narrow street! One of those old buildings! No, no. We couldn't insure that."

Next day Father Westphal and Carl visited more insurance agents in the city. Finally at the eleventh office, the agent agreed. Father paid the premium, and the agent gave him the papers.

"Now I'll feel better about the mission office and the printshop while I'm away on trips," he sighed.

Only a few days after Father Westphal left on a trip up north to the part of Chile that is a desert, there was a fire in that old building in Williams Passage. The workers were able to run to safety. They couldn't save anything from the office or the printshop.

When they told Mrs. Westphal about it, she sent her husband a telegram. And for a wonder it reached him. (Sometimes telegrams never do get through.) When he came home, he went promptly to the insurance agent, who paid for the loss. Now Father Westphal had almost enough money to buy and outfit a new press. They found a place with no buildings nearby. Mother felt much better about this new building.

Chapter 12

The family didn't stay long in the city of Valparaiso.

"I want my son to live in the country and learn to work like my brothers and I did," Father said to Mother and Carl after they had been living in Valparaiso for a while. "The city is no place for a boy."

Carl smiled and perked up his ears to listen.

Mother spoke up. "And I want my babies to live in the country too where they can have good milk and plenty of fresh air."

They had only one baby. Was there going to be another? Carl wondered.

Before he could ask, Father spoke up.

"I've decided—"

"We've decided," Mother corrected him.

Carl waited eagerly to hear this decision.

"We've decided to live in Pua [Pü a].

Carl thought that a very queer name for a place. That word meant a little twist of wire on a barbed-wire fence.

Mother explained that Pua was a small town farther south. "The country is very beautiful," she said. "A family by the name of Kriegoff lives there. They

have given land for a mission school."

Carl thought that sounded great—living in the country and going to a mission school.

The family went to Pua by train and then in a big Russian wagon just like the ones the farmers in Entre Ríos used to use.

Carl found the country beautiful all right, but he was disappointed about the mission school. It wasn't ready to start yet.

His father bought him a violin to cheer him. They found a teacher for him, and his mother insisted that he practice an hour every day. The squawks and squeaks that he made at first didn't sound like music. And the practice hour seemed very long.

Then one day Mother told Carl that they were expecting another baby in the family. The expected baby would arrive sometime in August.

At last the baby came, a little girl to keep Ruth company. But such a tiny, weak baby! She came in August, which is a really cold month in southern Chile.

To keep the little one warm they wrapped her in blankets. They then gently placed her in the oven of their big kitchen stove! Of course they left the oven door open. It was Carl's job to bring in the wood. The fire in the stove had to be kept just right to keep the oven not too warm, not too cold.

They named the little girl Grace Hazel. She grew stronger and bigger as the days went by. It was easy to see that she would be dark like her mother and Carl. Carl loved his little sister. But his big problem was that the mission school had not been opened.

How long would it be before Carl could go to the

5-G.L.B.

mission school? When would it open?

When Carl was sixteen, the mission school was completed and ready to open. There were only eight children who attended that first year. Mr. Kriegoff was the teacher and his wife the "school mother." Not enough money, not enough teachers, not even enough students. But they believed it would grow just as the school in Argentina had grown.

But there were no academy classes. That meant home study once more for Carl!

One day when Father was home for a few days, he and Carl were spading in the yard, preparing the ground for a garden. Carl looked up and saw the fence bending over. It seemed to be bowing to them. Father saw it too. They both ran to the house to see if all was well there. As they came through the door, they saw their hanging lamp swaying from side to side.

"An earthquake!" Father Westphal shouted.

Actually Carl and Mother and little Ruthie were used to little quakes. That day was the baby's birthday. Little Grace was one year old.

"That may have been a really bad earthquake somewhere else," Father warned them.

Sure enough! Telegraph lines were cut, but little by little they heard the terrible news. The city of Valparaiso, where they had once lived, was almost destroyed. How anxious they felt about their friends there! They wondered if the printing press and mission office had been ruined.

"I must go to Valparaiso at once!" Father insisted.

"Let me go with you," Carl begged. "I'm sixteen years old and I can help you."

"No," Father said. "You stay here and take care of our home and garden. You are needed here."

Valparaiso was more than 400 miles away. Elder Westphal was gone for two weeks. When he finally returned, they had a meeting in the church. He told what had happened.

"No one was allowed in the city for a week," Father told them. "So I had to wait a couple of days to get in. As I made my way through the ruined streets, I saw that most of the city's great buildings had collapsed. Everywhere houses were crumbled. Thousands of people had died. Thousands were crowded into the hospitals. Some of our church members had been hurt. Everywhere I saw people with pale, frightened faces. Many were without anything to eat. Where could they buy food with the stores all knocked down?

"Of course I went first," Elder Westphal said, "to the printshop and the mission office. I am glad to tell you that both were safe. God had cared for them. We were thankful the printing press was no longer in Williams Passage. That area was just a heap of ruins with people buried underneath.

"The mission and press workers had a special thanksgiving service. Since the printing press was not harmed by the earthquake, the men got out a special number of the *Signs of the Times*. It told the story of the earthquake. It showed that earthquakes were a sign of the end of our world and of Jesus' second coming."

Carl's father took a pile of the papers with him as he traveled north by ship. At each port he sold the papers. All he had to do was call out in a loud voice,

"Read about the earthquake in Valparaiso." People came running to get the news. It was the first magazine to tell the story. Even the newspapers hadn't been able to print anything because their presses were destroyed.

At one place a man began to shout, "Don't buy that trash! They teach that we should keep Saturday instead of Sunday!" His voice was louder than the missionary's, but it just called the attention of the people even more to the man who had the papers about the Valparaiso earthquake. When they heard "Read all about the earthquake!" they crowded around Elder Westphal. He sold all his *Signs* and wished he had brought more.

Chapter 13

The same year as the earthquake the family received exciting news. A letter from Uncle Joe and Aunt Jennie in Argentina brought the surprise. Their pretty daughter Flora was to be married. One of the ministers from Chile by the name of Eduardo Thomann had been visiting in their home. He was on his way to Paraguay to hold meetings. Uncle Joe wondered why he stayed so long. Why didn't he hurry on to Paraguay?

Then this Pastor Thomann got sick. The doctor operated on him for appendicitis. They used Aunt Jennie's kitchen table for an operating table. The doctor had taught Flora how to put the patients to sleep with chloroform. So Flora was giving the chloroform there in the kitchen. When Eduardo was going to sleep, he began to talk. He said he loved Flora! They all laughed and teased her. Uncle Joe said now he understood why Pastor Thomann stayed so long at their house.

"Flora is only eighteen," Mother Westphal remembered, "but she will make a good minister's wife. Eduardo is much older than Flora. He's 32. But they'll be a fine Christian couple. They are going to Bolivia to do mission work, the letter says."

"Is Pastor Thomann the one I've heard so many stories about?" Carl asked.

"Yes, indeed, he was very important in our mission work here in Chile in the early days," Father said. "He is Swiss. When he became an Adventist, he wanted everyone to know about the Sabbath and Jesus' coming. He wanted to spread the news all over.

"He and his brother went from house to house with papers. They walked the streets of Santiago [Sän' tē ä gō] until they wore out their shoes. Between them, they had only one pair left. Eduardo wore the shoes one day while his brother stayed home to study the Bible. Next day his brother wore the shoes and Eduardo stayed home to study the Bible. So the brothers shared one pair of shoes.

"In those days most Adventist books and papers were in English or German. Eduardo Thomann needed more tracts and papers in Spanish. He decided to write some himself. He learned English. He translated whole books into Spanish. He became a printer. After he had printed the papers that he wrote, he sold them. He sold them in Santiago, the capital city of Chile, and he sold them in Peru and in Bolivia."

"What a man!" Carl exclaimed. "Writer, printer, salesman. He was a publishing company all by himself."

"One time he was in a certain city in Chile," Father went on. "He worked all morning selling his magazines. At noon he went into a restaurant to eat. He laid his book bag by the door. After eating, he missed the bag. Someone had stolen it. Inside the bag was his Bible and the books and magazines he was selling.

"Eduardo Thomann took a ship right back to Valparaiso where there was a small Adventist print shop. In Valparaiso he wrote and printed more papers. A year later he went back to the city where his books had been stolen.

"One day a lady stepped up to him. 'Are you selling the *Signs of the Times?*' she asked.

" 'Yes, and other books and magazines too.' he answered.

"Then she asked him to wait a minute. She disappeared. Soon she came back with some books, papers, and a Bible and asked, 'Do these belong to you?'

" 'Yes, they surely do!' Eduardo said after looking at them. 'But where did you find them?'

" 'I'm sorry to confess it, but I stole them,' the woman said. 'I thought the bag might have jewels in it. Then I found only papers and books. Nothing of value, or so I thought. Then I noticed the Bible was full of marks. I thought it must be something important after all. So I read and read and studied and studied. Now I am keeping the Sabbath and looking for Jesus.'

"She looked at Eduardo Thomann anxiously. 'I know I did wrong to steal your books. Will you forgive me?'

"What could he say? He was most happy.

" 'There really were jewels in your bag,' the lady said smiling at Eduardo."

Carl thought it would be great to have Eduardo Thomann for a cousin.

Chapter 14

Soon Carl had to leave home and move into Santiago to continue his studies. He lived there with friends while going to school. He hadn't forgotten that he wanted to be a doctor.

Chile is called the Shoestring Republic because it is long and narrow. It is just a strip of land between the Pacific Ocean and the Andes Mountains. That meant that Elder Westphal had to travel either north or south most of the time. Santiago was in the center of the country, so he often saw Carl on his journeys.

Carl found his father always cheerful, always working hard, always trying to save money for the mission.

Several times Elder Westphal had visited a certain man in northern Chile. When this man moved to the southern part of the country, he told his friends and relatives about Adventists. They wanted to know more. Elder Westphal decided to visit the man in southern Chile, but he lived forty-two miles from the nearest railroad station.

Another man went with Elder Westphal. They traveled by train as far as possible. At the last railroad station they could have hired horses or a horse and wagon. They thought they ought not to spend the money because they had so little. One o'clock in the afternoon they started to walk the forty-two miles. Surely they could find a farmer who would let them stay all night at his place.

There were so many robbers in that part of the country that the farmers were afraid to take in two strangers. So at dusk they had to turn aside to sleep in the woods. There they made a cheerful fire and lay down to sleep beside it. Both men were wearing long coats, called dusters. In the night Elder Westphal's duster got too near the fire. He wasn't burned himself, but his long duster was burned and ruined. He had to travel the rest of the way without a coat.

Next day they arrived in Canete [Cä nē'tē] and received a warm welcome from friends. Every evening for two weeks they held meetings. Before leaving Elder Westphal baptized eighteen.

Very early on the morning after the baptism they started back so they could walk the forty-two miles in one day. They made it! But they were too tired to sleep that night.

Next time Carl's father went to Canete, he went alone. He bought a pair of *alpargatas* [äl pär gät' os] to wear instead of shoes. They are slippers made with canvas tops. The sole is made of braided rope. The country people love their *alpargatas*. Elder Westphal found them light and airy.

Again he decided to walk the forty-two miles to save money. This time he found a hotel on the way where he could sleep. Next morning when he put on his slippers, he felt as if he were standing on marbles. A look at his feet showed why. The soles of his feet were covered with great big blisters. He put paper into the slippers and started out. But every step caused him pain. People looked at him strangely as he limped along.

As he climbed the mountains, every once in a while he would pass a cross by the roadside. In Chile that meant that someone had been killed there.

Suddenly a man jumped out of the woods and ran after Elder Westphal. The missionary had to forget all about the blisters on his feet, and run as fast as he could. He outran the man who chased him. Elder Westphal stopped where some men were working. He told them about the fellow who had scared him. Just then the man came running around the corner.

"That's the man!" Elder Westphal shouted.

The men laughed."That's the village idiot!" they told him. "He can't hurt anybody."

Upon arriving at Canete, his friends welcomed him. When they saw his feet, they said, "You really love us. We thank you for coming to teach us more of the Bible. We won't forget what you did for us."

And again he baptized some more people before leaving.

Chapter 15

Father Westphal decided to buy a farm out in the country, fifty miles from the mission school in Pua. The family couldn't be there all the time, because Father still traveled all over and held meetings. Mother Westphal taught at the school in Pua, and the little girls went to school there too. Carl could only be home from college in Santiago for vacations. But what fun they had when it was possible for the family to be together at the farm.

The whole family made quite a fuss over Carl when he could join them. Mother made all the special dishes that Carl liked so much.

There was plenty of work for Carl when he could be home. Even the girls, Ruth the blonde and Grace the little brunette, could help. A favorite pastime was scaring the bees away while someone got the honey. Armed with kitchen spoons and kettles, they formed a tin-pan army with real kettledrums. The honey from the Westphal farm was very special, very mild and white. Whenever Father made a trip to Argentina to attend meetings there, he took some to Uncle Joe's family.

At one time when Carl and his father were both on the farm, Carl talked to his father about his future.

He still wanted to be a doctor.

"Father, I have heard there is a new medical school being opened in Loma Linda, California. Do you think I could attend that college?"

Father said, "Yes, Son, if you want to go, we will make every effort to help you. It will cost lots of money, but you could work, and we would manage somehow."

"But, if I took my medical course in the United States, wouldn't it be hard for me to get permission to practice medicine in South America?"

"Yes, that's very true," Father Westphal nodded.

"Well," continued Carl, "since I want to be a missionary doctor in South America, wouldn't it be better to study medicine here?"

His father was thoughtful. "I've thought a lot about that, Son. You know the language for studying in Spanish. There is a good medical college in Santiago. You would be a more useful doctor for the Lord's work if you took your course here. There's just one thing that is against it."

"And what's that?" Carl asked.

"I understand the classes are held six days a week. It would be almost impossible for you to pass the classes without going to school on Sabbaths."

Carl said he had thought of that also, but he had made up his mind that he could do it—with God's help.

"We would rather not have you be a doctor than to have you break the Sabbath," Father told him.

"I promise you, Father, that I will be faithful to God, no matter what happens."

Carl wished his mother, who was not well, could

go to the United States again to see a good doctor and be in an Adventist sanitarium. He often wished his little sisters could visit the homeland too. But there was no chance. Father had made one trip when he was invited to attend a General Conference. At the time he had thought he would see his old father. But his father had died just before he reached America. Carl remembered the United States well, but his little sisters knew nothing about it.

When they talked about it, Mother always said how lucky they were to live in Chile where they had such a good climate. She always added, "And there are good fruits and vegetables here. Many missionaries aren't as fortunate as we are."

One time when Father Westphal returned home after a tiring trip, Ruth and Grace climbed on his knee and asked for a story. Carl, who happened to be at home at the time, sat down near his father. He had never gotten over his love for listening to his father's stories.

He told them about the time he had walked twenty-seven miles in one day with Victor Thomann, the brother of their cousin Eduardo. After that long walk they still had four more miles to go. It was getting dark. It had been raining hard, so the road was full of mudholes—big ones. The water came up to their knees, and up to their shoulders in some places.

At last the two men had to climb up on a roadside fence. They crawled along on the top rail. They struggled on through the muddy water. When they came to the place where Elder Westphal thought the house should be, he looked around. Not a thing in sight! He began to shout loudly. Soon a voice answered. They found the voice was that of the very man they were looking for!

The man made his muddy friends welcome to his home. The men stayed to study with some people. Before leaving six people were baptized, and a little Sabbath School started.

Father laughed. "The next time I went to that town I rode horseback for those twenty-seven miles.

"The horse stopped and looked at each big mudhole. He seemed to be thinking whether or not he wanted to go in," Father said. "There were bags of books hanging around the horse's neck besides the usual saddle bags on his back. At one place the poor horse got stuck in a deep hole."

"What did you do, Papa?" little Grace asked.

"My dear, I stood up on the horse's back and jumped to a log. Then I found that fence again and climbed up on the top rail to crawl along."

"And the horse, Papa?"

"Oh, once I jumped off his back, he was able to get out of the mud."

"What about the books?" Ruth asked.

"Well, they were pretty wet, but they weren't ruined. The people were very happy to get them anyway.

"Another time when I was riding a horse as he floundered through the mudholes, I suddenly found myself and the horse plunged into a deep hole that totally submerged the horses body, only his ears stuck up. I was in up to my waist." Father chuckled as he remembered. "You know, the people looked at

79

me strangely as I walked into town, covered with mud. Had the Adventist minister become a bandit? Or had he been attacked by robbers? they must have wondered.

"I think the people came to the meetings just to see what was the matter with me!" Father Westphal laughed. "Anyway, it was good advertising."

Carl grinned at his father as he said, "Your beard is gray now instead of blond, but you certainly do get around. You're quite a cowboy!"

The family laughed, thinking of Father as a South American gaucho.

Chapter 16

Elder Westphal had just received a letter.

"Who is it from?" Mother Westphal asked.

"It's from a man I've never met," Father said as he opened the letter and began to read. "He wants to know more about Adventists, and he wants me to visit him."

"Where does he live?" Mother Westphal asked.

"That's the problem. I never heard of the place before. I have no idea where it is."

Elder Westphal kept asking friends where that certain town was, but no one had ever heard of it.

"Papa, you have the man's address. You'll just have to write and ask where that place is," Ruth suggested.

"Good thinking, little girl. That's what I'll do."

The man answered the letter Father Westphal wrote. He told Elder Westphal to go to San Jose by train on a certain day. San Jose was a very small town north and east of Pua. There he promised to meet Elder Westphal with some horses and take him to the village.

When Elder Westphal got off the train, he wondered how he would know the man. He didn't need to worry. The man knew him right away—dark suit,

gray beard, bag of books. That had to be the Adventist preacher. The man came up to him, and after greeting him he took him to where the horses stood waiting. They mounted the two horses and rode fast across the plains. Then they came to the mountains—and such mountains!

"You won't be able to guide your horse on this mountain trail," the man told Father Westphal. "Just leave the reins loose, and let the horse choose the way."

A cliff rose high above one side of the path, and on the other was a deep rocky canyon. The horse chose his way carefully, stepping first this way and then that way among the rocks. Elder Westphal kept praying for the horse.

After some hours they came into a beautiful little valley. There was the man's farm. No one else lived close by.

"Where's the village?" the missionary asked.

The man pointed to a little river that ran through the valley. "That river runs down to the village on the coast. I'll take you there tomorrow," he promised.

When they rode their horses down into the town the next day, they found a group of people keeping the Sabbath and looking for Jesus to come again.

The missionary asked what minister had visited them.

"No one," his friend said. "We have been studying by ourselves."

The man had been a sexton in the village Catholic church. A sexton is one who rings the church bells. Of course he had attended that church and knew the priest well.

A little tugboat came into the port one day. The people in the village all gathered around to see the boat. The sexton saw that the captain was reading a book.

"What book is that?" he asked.

The captain told him it was a Bible.

"May I borrow it for a little while?" the sexton asked. "I never saw a Bible before."

The captain gladly let him take the Book home to read.

Somehow the village priest found out that the sexton was reading the Bible. He didn't like to have the man who rang his church bells reading the Bible.

The priest sent a messenger to the sexton saying, "I have bought the Bible from the captain, and I want to have it."

The sexton went to ask the captain if he had really sold the Bible to the priest.

"No, I haven't sold it," he answered. "If you want to buy it, I'll give you first chance."

The sexton bought the Bible quickly and began to read it. Then one of his relatives gave him some Adventist papers. Not long afterward there was a little group of believers in the area. They learned whole chapters of the Bible by heart. When they got hymnbooks, they memorized the words of sixty songs.

It seemed to Elder Westphal that the family on the farm where he stayed got up very early in the morning.

"These people are up and are having worship while I am still in bed," he said to himself. "I must get up earlier tomorrow and join them."

The next morning he heard them singing still earlier before he was up.

"How does it happen you get up so early to have worship?" he asked the farmer. "I hear you singing while it is still dark."

Then they told him they weren't out of bed yet when he heard them singing.

"Whenever the rooster crows, we sing and pray. Then we go back to sleep again."

No wonder they got ahead of the missionary every day!

Chapter 17

When Elder Westphal traveled back and forth, north and south of Santiago where Carl attended medical school, he often stopped to visit his son. On one of his visits he said to Carl, "Well, at last, Son, I'm finally going to go way down south to Punta Arenas."

"How many years have you been hoping to go and talking about it?" Carl asked.

"Fourteen years," Father Westphal answered. "Fourteen years since I went by ship through the Straits of Magellan. That was the year I came to Chile, 1904. I always hoped after that to go back to Punta Arenas."

"Has anyone ever gone there to preach the gospel?" Carl asked.

"Oh, yes. As always, the book salesmen went first. Also Brother Arthur Nelson and his wife are there now."

"Well," Carl smiled at his father, "be sure to take your long red flannel underwear."

Father Westphal laughed. "I already have it packed. I know it's cold down there." Then Father became serious. He spoke sadly. "Your mother isn't well, Carl. She may need you while I am away. In fact you may need to bring her here with you where she can see a good doctor."

"Now, don't worry; I'll take care of Mother," Carl promised.

Elder Westphal left his son and started on his trip south. He was away for five months, and during that time Mrs. Westphal did get very sick. Telegrams were sent to Elder Westphal asking him to come home, but the journey back took nearly a month. In the meantime, Carl decided to move the family to Santiago, where his mother could have good medical care and he could look after her. He found a house in the city where he moved the family, and he went to live with them.

Elder Westphal hurried home as fast as possible. He went straight to the farm where he had left the family. There he found a locked, empty house. Friends told him where Mrs. Westphal and the girls had gone.

"I'm glad you moved the family to the city where you could be near Mother and the girls and Mother could have the medical help she needs," Father Westphal told Carl. "We'll stay here for a while. I can serve as pastor of the church along with my other duties." Father said, adding, "The girls can study here too."

"The best part," Carl said, "is that I can live at home and finish my medical college work."

That evening the family gathered around Father Westphal, eager to hear about the meetings he had held in Punta Arenas.

"Was it easy?" one of the girls asked.

"No," Father Westphal replied slowly. "It wasn't

an easy place to work. Sometimes there were very few people at the meetings. But I kept on." He laughed and then said, "In fact, one night only one person came to the meeting. Just one woman! I preached the sermon just for her alone. It proved to be well worthwhile, though, because after that she brought her two sons with her to the meetings. I feel sure those boys will become preachers someday. Her husband was very much against her. He burned the Bible she had in the house. She also had a copy of *The Great Controversy* that she kept hidden away. After her husband went to sleep each night, she got up and read from the book until she had finished it."

"How many people did you baptize?" Carl wanted to know.

"Nine! Nine new church members," Father Westphal answered with a happy smile.

Many times during the years the Westphals lived in Chile, Elder Westphal had to cross the high Andes mountains to go to Argentina to attend special meetings there. The first two times he went, he rode on the back of a mule. At times he got off the mule's back and walked a ways, but whenever he did that he had trouble breathing. The mountains were so high that the air was thin and it was hard for a person to breathe.

Later, when a railroad was built, Elder Westphal traveled by train. The train went through a tunnel that had been made through the highest part of the mountain. On the snowy summit between the countries of Argentina and Chile there is a beautiful statue. It is a figure of Jesus with his hands outstretched in blessing. He seems to be keeping peace between the two countries. The statue is called *The Christ of the Andes.* It is made of canons and canon balls that were melted down. It was made to be a sign of the promise that there will be no more war between Argentina and Chile.

Every time Elder Westphal returned from Argentina to Chile, his family noticed how red and swollen his face had become. He always developed an allergy rash when in Argentina.

Several years before the family had moved to Chile, Elder Westphal had spent a couple of weeks there. He had stayed with a family who were interested in everything he had to say about the Bible. Before each meal he studied with them. The mother became a faithful Seventh-day Adventist, and she remained faithful through the years.

Now, many years later when Carl was attending medical school in that city, he often met this woman at prayer meeting. She seemed to have a great burden, and one day, with tears in her eyes, she said to Carl, "Please, please, pray for my daughter." For several weeks she kept asking Carl to remember her daughter in prayer.

Then one night she seemed very sad. "My daughter left home. She has gone to Argentina to get a job. She left home because she didn't want to hear any more about the Sabbath. Please pray for her," the mother again asked Carl.

For five years that mother was always praying that her daughter would come home and keep the Sabbath again.

One Wednesday evening the mother seemed happy. "My daughter is coming home!" she told

Carl, her eyes sparkled. "Do keep on praying for her."

But a couple of weeks later the mother seemed sad again. "She went away," she told Carl, "this time to southern Chile. She is very angry that I am still faithful. When she found that her sister-in-law is also an Adventist, she was still more upset. She packed up and left at once."

"Please pray for her, Carl," the mother said every Wednesday evening. "Your father brought us the gospel, so you must help with your prayers."

His prayers and hers were being answered in a strange way. The daughter got sick. She couldn't sleep and she couldn't eat. Her doctor found nothing wrong with her.

Then the girl had a dream. An angel told her she should return to Santiago. That wasn't what she wanted to do at all, so she stayed on, but she didn't get well.

Again she saw the angel. This time he was seated on a white horse. His beautiful wings were spread out. "You should go to Santiago immediately. Do not delay," he said.

Next morning she packed her trunk and went to the port to get a ship. The boat had already left. She would have to wait a week for the next ship.

During that week the angel came to her again. "Be of good cheer!" he told her. Then he showed her a group of people praying and singing. She also saw a preacher with a red face. "That man will teach you," the angel said.

By this time the Westphal family had moved to Santiago and were always at church.

When the young woman came home, her sister-in-law wanted to invite her to church. "But," she thought, "there's no use. She has left home two times to get away from the Sabbath." But after praying about it, she dared to say, "Would you like to go to Sabbath School and church with me tomorrow?"

When the girl said Yes, the sister-in-law could hardly believe her ears. Of course she didn't know at that time about the dream and the angel.

The next day the girl went to church. Services were in an old theater. When the daughter saw the place and the people, she said to her mother, "This is the very place the angel showed me, and the same people too." Then she told about her dream.

Elder Westphal, who had recently returned from a trip to Argentina, and Carl weren't at church that Sabbath because there was a baptism to be held in another place. But the next Sabbath Elder Westphal met the young lady at the door of the church.

"You are the man with the red face!" she exclaimed. "An angel let me see you and told me you would help me."

Elder Westphal's face, as usual, after being in Argentina was red and swollen. It was a solemn moment when he and the girl met. Then they had to laugh about his red face. The angel knew it would still be red when the girl met him!

Her health? Oh, yes, she got well fast.

Chapter 18

Father, mother, Ruth, and Grace all felt proud of Carl who was soon to become a full-fledged doctor. He had studied for twelve years in Santiago, always facing the problem of keeping the Sabbath. Classes were held six days a week. Sometimes examinations came on Sabbath or on Friday night. These were usually oral tests. The names of the students were listed in alphabetical order. Since *Westphal* came near the end of the alphabet, Carl was able to trade places with someone whose name came near the beginning. That way he could take his test a day earlier if necessary.

Then it came time for him to take his final examination in medicine. After that he would be a doctor. The tests were given in the evening. His classmates asked Carl what he would do if he had to appear on Friday evening.

"I just hope and pray it won't happen," he answered. But it did happen just that way.

One of the teachers said, "Carl, why don't you go early for your test. We'll ask you a lot of questions first. Then after sundown you can perhaps just sit there with your arms folded."

Carl knew the other teachers would not do the

same, and he felt it would not be the right way to keep the Sabbath.

How the family prayed those days! In fact, the whole Santiago church prayed about it.

"I would rather see you fail to graduate than to have you fail to be true to God," his father told him. "You are going to pass a test that is even more important than your medical examination."

"God is testing you," his mother reminded him.

Carl stayed away from the examination. He and his family spent the time in prayer. Not to take that examination was to fail in his medical course. To fail after all his years of study! After all the money his parents had spent on his education! Sabbath was a sad day. But Carl felt close to Jesus.

Sunday morning the newspapers printed the names of the students who had passed the examinations. Of course his name was not among them.

Monday morning he went to talk to the secretary of the medical college.

"You will be allowed to take the examinations on another day," he was told. "When the teachers knew you had not taken the examination because of your belief and faith, they took the matter to the board of education."

What rejoicing there was! What an answer to prayer! On Sabbath while the church prayed, the board of education had made that decision.

Soon Carl could sign his name with M.D. after it.

Times had changed during the years the Westphals were in Chile. Missionary children could return to the homeland to study. Their parents would have regular furloughs, or vacation trips, back to the United States. Ruth and Grace were young teenagers when Carl graduated from medicine. They both wanted to be nurses. So Elder and Mrs. Westphal and the two girls sailed back to the United States. Carl chose to stay in South America to be a missionary himself. He didn't know whether he would ever see his family again.

Elder Westphal, who had been the first Adventist minister in South America, now became the first pastor of a Spanish church in California. They lived in Glendale where the girls attended the academy and took their nurses' training. That was a dream come true for Ruth and Grace.

Another dream came true for Carl in South America. He was asked to go back to Entre Ríos where he had loved to visit as a boy. There a hospital had been built beside the college. He spent the rest of his life right there in medical mission work. He was proud to carry on the family tradition of missionary work, proud to have been the son of a trailblazer of the gospel in South America.